The Remedies

KATHARINE TOWERS was born in London and read
Modern Languages at St. Hilda's College, Oxford. Her first
collection, *The Floating Man*, won the Seamus Heaney Centre
Prize for Poetry, and was shortlisted for both the Aldeburgh First
Collection Prize and the Ted Hughes Award, as well as being
longlisted for the *Guardian* First Book Award. She lives in
the Peak District with her husband and two daughters.

Katharine Towers

The Remedies

PICADOR

First published 2016 by Picador
an imprint of Pan Macmillan,
20 New Wharf Road, London N1 9RR
Associated companies throughout the world
www.panmacmillan.com

ISBN 978-1-5098-1305-6

3 5 7 9 8 6 4 2

A CIP catalogue record for this book is available from the British Library.

Printed and bound by CPI Group (UK) Ltd, Croydon, CR0 4YY

Visit **www.picador.com** to read more about all our books
and to buy them. You will also find features, author interviews and
news of any author events, and you can sign up for e-newsletters
so that you're always first to hear about our new releases.

For Andy and Bluebell and Daisy

ACKNOWLEDGEMENTS

Some of these poems or versions of them were
first published in *Poetry Review*, *Poetry London*,
13 Pages, *The North* and *In Your Own Time*.

My thanks to dear friends at the Northern Poetry
Workshop, my editor Don Paterson and to the
NCLA's Poetics of the Archive project.

Contents

III

Beauty is momentary in the mind

— Wallace Stevens

Je suis belle, ô mortels! comme un rêve de pierre

— Baudelaire

I

The Roses

Because my father will not stand again
beneath these swags of *Himalayan Musk*
nor stare for hours to see which stems are safe

and which need tying back, I have it in my mind
to let the roses pull our house down slowly
for a hundred years. Then I'll come back

to find its wreck of thorns and brick, my father
lying on the bed in which he died
and blinking in the petal-scented light.

Porcelain

clay rears up
wavering towards its shape
headstrong and fragile

as the new-born fawn
swaying at her mother's flank
uncertain and certain

The Grasshopper

Origami made him from a leaf
folded into minute symmetries

of eye and wing, long hind legs
fitted for leaping and music-making.

One day he elbowed his way up
out of the mire to sing of love

and of his perfectly broken heart —
O, such meagre tinder for a fire!

The Chaffinch

His endless *chink chink*.
Pity his obsession:
all he knows is that he is
and he must say so.
If once or twice he is amazed
his song will never vary –
he cannot rise to art
and no-one has told him
he always sounds the same.
Never bored, he understands
that moments must be uttered
and moments do not matter –
there will always be more
and there is no death.
Hear him on his high twig
in this summer rain.

Murmuration

Take these birds, arriving from
the corners of the moor
or blowing from the trees like leaves.

We're all here to be amazed and stare
as they try out the sky,
rehearsing every version of *multitude*.

Someone finds a freak wave, smoke
without a fire; another sees a soul adrift
in the dusk . . . Though none of this is about us.

The starlings clatter down
blackening the stems of bulrushes and reeds.

Childhood

These criss-cross lines printed on the snow
are bones of trees laid bare by the moon.
We should not be looking so hard

at what a tree would rather keep to itself.
Would we not fear to be shown
how like replicas we are, and how mechanical?

Let's play that game again, stepping out
along the branches – pretending to tip –
as if we still believed we couldn't fall.

rain

if we stand in woods after rain when the trees are iron and purple, like wine, we'll wish we could stay – not to wait for the woollen comfort of dusk, nor to hear the wind flinching back from the heart to let it be quiet and still . . . but to stand in the iron and purple of evening, our stories behind us like toys we've forgotten or lost, till we enter at last that place in the heart (that place in the dark of the heart) where there's nothing, not even weather

The Glass Piano

No, I did not swallow or inhale the glass piano.
It has grown inside me like a crystal in salt water
or an alien cell, accreting keys and string after string
until one day I reached the full eight octaves.
Some days I'm loud. I growl bass chords
or sigh chromatically from A to middle C,
play a waltz or gigue until notes hurtle from my skin.
Still, I keep my distance. Clasped or grasped I'll shatter
endlessly with every lovely theme and variation.

Field Oak

the riddled bark
the sap that seals the broken heart
the staggered reach
the secret passed from leaf to leaf
the stalwart roots
the tiny chalices of fruit
the watercolours of the dusk
the tried-and-tested triplets of a thrush

So Beautiful it Must be True

'It's enough if a single note is played perfectly' – Arvo Pärt

One day a note flew up and landed in your heart.
It settled in between the lisping chambers,

singing to itself and wanting only
to be left alone – *no eavesdropping!*

It tiptoed up and down your arteries
leaving echoes in corners and a hum.

Fearing it was gone, you wept until you felt
a familiar pain like a bruise to the groin.

When it flew away you wept again,
bathing your perfect invisible wound.

Tinnitus

If only it were church bells
or the early morning chanting
of a choir of boys in Latin.

You could even learn to love
your own inner sea –
swishing through the ossicles,

but not this round-the-clock
back-chat of an irritated nerve
that doesn't know it's time to shut up.

Conversation isn't what you miss
as you stare out at the garden,
palms pressed against the glass.

Daisies

We don't wish to shout
or be brilliant or climb up walls
or hang from walls

but to sit in the grass
in our clean best frills and listen,
shyly nodding our heads
or shyly shaking our heads
because we understand, yes truly we do.

At the Villa of the Papyri, Herculaneum

Do you wonder what causes lightning, earthquakes and eclipses?
What if there were natural explanations for the things that terrify you?
Do you fear that the mighty gods are angry?
Have you ever felt safe in a city without walls?

Is it virtuous to devote one's life to the pursuit of truth?
Is debate with an intellectual equal more or less useful than solitary contemplation?
Do you long for the flimsy pleasures of wealth and renown (honestly)?
What's wrong with a humble existence surviving on bread, water and pots of cheese?

Do you believe in the immortal soul?
Have you tried imagining the soul as part of the body – like the mouth?
Have you ever said out loud things you knew not to be true?

Are you frankly bored to death at home?
Do you fear that the mighty gods are angry?
Do you feel sorrow when you hear these words: atom; void?

undulatus asperitas

Once we saw a great cloud, made of ice
like any other cloud but wind-sheared
and drooping in the heavy air.
It lolled against the hill but no storm fell.
Barometers dropped like stones and it was
purple-dark, even in the early afternoon.
The ruckled sky had us standing pointing
in the fields like scarecrows, and mostly afraid.

Girls fainted under the weight of ions
and some of us made thankful prayers
for the wonder of that rolling sea above.
They say that waves from underneath
are kind and do not mean us harm –
even seem to love us; and it's bliss to drown.

Saints

'Visitors can crank Landy's recycled saints
into life with a foot pedal mechanism.'

– National Gallery catalogue

This one beats the rungs of his chest
with a clockwork fist and turns away
his harrowed, tin-plate face.

Saint Catherine ticks round and round
on her ramshackle wheel.
You can spin her faster with this handle

or press a switch so Apollonia's eyelids click
as she circles the meagre stack
that is her own snapped-out teeth.

Shiny paper makes the wounds
of poor Saint Francis: he'll wince
and weep, if you dare to touch.

Dear saints! Let them not endure to the last.
All they are is human flesh.
By which I mean rag-and-bone.

August

Crickets ticking in the long grass know
what we don't. There's not much time.

On this day without a point we lie
and watch the clouds go by.

We can't live like clocks and feel
the ache of every stroke.

Grass

If I were called in
to construct a religion
I should make use of grass.

Going to church
would entail a fervent swishing
through couch and wild oats.

My liturgy would employ
vegetal whistling
and blurted worshipful shrieks.

And I should be
a singer of grass, spitting all
but the sweetest pith from my mouth.

Whim Wood

into the coppery halls
of beech and intricate oak
to be close to the trees
as they whisper together
let fall their leaves,
and we die for the winter

II

Flower Remedies

Agrimony

– a remedy for mental torture that is kept hidden

All summer I cough up
umpteen tiny yellow blooms.

I can't help looking cheerful
but in my heart of hearts

I'm troubled.
If I could choose I'd bear

a single dark blue flower –
heavy as a stone, and bitter-scented.

Aspen

— a remedy for fear of the unknown

Naturally we're phobic,
each afraid of everything.

When the wind gets up
we enact a delicate hysteria —

our leaf-hearts startle
and we fibrillate beautifully.

Water Violet

— a remedy for those who are proud and disdainful

I hold my head above the spate
to keep my thoughts dry.

I wonder if I'm lonely or if this half-
drowned life is good enough.

All night I stand on my dignity
as I gaze up, star-struck.

Early Gentian

– a remedy for low spirits and dejection

My grief is that I'm beautiful.
I peel apart to show
the velvet violet of my throat

and though I cannot sing
I'm equal to this note of sadness
dark among the threads of grass.

Willow

– a remedy for self-pity

Don't think that I weep.
I'm practising drowning.

I'll do it one leaf at a time,
a meticulous immersion.

The river rises and falls
and makes no difference –

water is always upon me
like a bad thought.

For all the good I have not done . . .
Forgive me, forgive me.

Cherry Plum

— a remedy for fear of insanity

A relic species making do
in a hedge of wildings and weeds,

I don't belong on this rackety
slope between parishes.

I flower in cold weather,
brittle stems that fall too soon.

But I could lose my head in spring —
in that sudden mad mayhem!

Hornbeam

– a remedy for apathy

A rumbling in the bones
but I'm too tired for spring.
All winter I have been
as good as dead.

This late light daunts me.
Birds are a trouble.
I will eat my own greenwood.
I will stay put.

Rock Rose

– a remedy for terror

I can't look down
from this chalky brink.

As I cling, I listen
to the large sea

rummaging for where
the cliffs are soft, or thin.

Holly

– a remedy for hatred and jealousy

I'm expert in subtle vexations.
I can stitch a thread of blood.

You see I can't love.
My dark green heart is good for nothing.

Always trotting out this same old hard-luck story . . .
Don't cry or I'll scratch out your eyes.

Clematis

– a remedy for those who dream too much

I have mastered this old wall
to look into the future
which is only garden upon garden.

In winter when I should be dead
I long for purple heat and bees.

My thoughts won't rest . . . O why
can't I settle for less?

Common Centaury

– a remedy for those who are too selfless

All summer long
I acquiesce –
a drudgery
of red and pink.

My flowers make
the grasses sing!
I'm only happy
when I'm saying *yes*.

Dog Rose

– a remedy for those whose lives lack direction

I'd love to talk out loud
but I only ramble under my breath
along an old brick wall –

except in summer when
I blurt out in brilliant pink
things I don't mean.

Chicory

— a remedy for possessive or selfish love

No-one loves as much as I
the brazen heads
of hawk's-beard and ox-tongue.

Gorgeous familiars . . . I need
your yellow yellow
to prove the blue of my blue!

Wild Balsam

– a remedy for impatience

I gave short shrift
to motherhood and flung
my children from me.
Who'd have those tiny shoots
under their feet all day?

I want to think and work.
I want to make of my hamstrung life
a brilliant fever.

III

The Window

Standing at the window staring out
at no-one or at nothing was my mother,
anxious for a homecoming.
I hurried home all night, until I woke.
She stayed with me that morning,
silent as a child who's sad or cold,
then dwindled like a hope until
by evening she had died again.
All night I stood beside my window
catching cold and staring out
at nothing or at no-one coming home.

Midnight

for AE

This darkness lit by one bird's
threadbare song.

Let's stand and listen, love.
No-one knows we're gone.

A Plate

Observe my delicate Koong-See, whey-faced
beside the lattice fence and warming
in her palm my gift of an ivory bead.

Inside the garden's midnight blue,
the apple tree lets fall its fruit
as Koong-See walks and thinks of love.

Close by, the suitor's tilting barge,
his chests of gold and jade
which turn the mandarin's head,

and here the drunken duke waving
his horsehair whip as we tiptoe
from the wedding feast across the bridge.

The stippled willow leaves –
how like the feathers of our souls
as we fly from the painted rim!

Iceberg Season

The icebergs arrive in their beautiful veils.
They drift along the aisles
of the sound with creaks and growls

seeking a warmth that will finish them.
We gather on cliff-tops to see them
and wonder at their overhangs

which birds love; kittiwakes and gulls
run amok, tricked into thinking
they've found a new home.

They are in our sights for weeks –
a gentle company that's bolder
when the moon is old and curdled

and keeps us all from sleep. As long as
they are with us we believe, and we weep
as we pray to the god of cold.

Nerval and the Lobster

His beautiful clatter turns heads.
I explain: he does not bark.
He knows the secrets of the sea.

He is docile at my heel
and slender as a mayfly.
He moves like a long blue bone.

I ask: what are you thinking,
elegant prince? Whisper what you remember.
What are you thinking, my brother?

The Palais-Royal is filling with ocean.
Salt frosts the golden halls.
Is this your work, O beautiful monster?

Brise Marine

An original converses with its translation

VERSO

For years we've been engrossed
in this colloque sentimental.
I suppose we must be soulmates.

Centuries ago – hearing the voices of sailors
singing far from land –
I brought them to you on a salt breeze . . .

Mon cœur! There's so much more I want to tell you.
Come close: we'll do this seul à seule
and whisper in a language no-one understands.

RECTO

I wonder what you see in me –
pale echo of your bracing amour fou.
Iles noyées, hope's farewell

lie far beyond my speech; if there's anything
to bind us it's the ennui of shipwreck
and a worn-out soul.

These words where I dwell are merely
figments of a mind. I would love you
if I could, mon pauvre cœur . . . Pauvre amoureux!

LOQUITUR LIBER

Eavesdropper for years on this va-et-vient
of love and amour rebuté, I know it all
by heart: the sailors' hapless melodies,

the tedium of endless passion. I go between
the weathers of their languages, shivering
to her froideur or burning in his heat.

This limbo is a tricky stance: je les aime
tous deux de tout mon cœur.
I can't speak it without feeling.

El Desdichado

On failing to translate Nerval

Not that I had wished to meet the Widower
nor any man who calls himself the Unconsoled.
But there he was, stepping from the wreckage of his tower,
harp pressed against his dusty heart.

He's dead, of course, but not beyond desiring
the flower that will comfort him,
a view of the sea where Posillipo leans down
and an arbour of roses to sit under.

Anyone can dream in the element of water.
We simply let its burly chords assuage us,
though few will trust its tunes for long.

And although he'll never truly live –
not as he once lived in that other language –
I've heard the tearful music of his lyre.

First Frost

See how frost enunciates the day –
spelling out each grass by name, each leaf and twig,
the petals of this stem of lady's smock.

The river's tongue is tied, its language daunted
by a clear-cut morning
on which I hold nothing but this breath.

Pilgrim

Think of the mole in his crib of earth,
blind to the truth,
lifting his hands in prayer.

Ballet

Balanced on a single note, she isn't real.
She'll break without music,
spilling tulle and sequins at our feet

like the sunburnt lizard, slinking
from the mosaic of her brilliant skin
and hurrying away to hide.

Two Toads

On a stone in the dark brown syrup of
pond he clambers and clasps
her and his arms round her neck
are like babies' and
his chin is a dream of breath on
her back and this is such
bliss – for she is as love-struck as
he is and she croaks so he knows that this
boneless softness together is
world without end for ever and ever amen.

Sequoia

I creep inside your old and fire-scathed heart.
Harboured by our common cause
of time and loss
I am exactly human in the dark.

Bluebells

In the way that we cannot be other
than ourselves even in the deep of winter
these woods where bluebells grow

are always bluebell woods.
The blunt grey tips poke up
through the melted leaf-litter.

They are entering their domain
and the light is startling to them.
They quietly jostle to get more of it.

It may be that they are concentrating
on making the blue they remember
or perhaps it will astound them.

Then they can do nothing except look
down at the earth, which is not a mirror,
learning thoughts of bluebells in a dark wood.

for example

if you stare in winter
at a leftover flower
in its clock of frost –
a rose, say, or a Japanese
anemone – you'll see
there's no need after all
to be afraid of dying

Notes

The Glass Piano

The poem arises from the true story of Princess Alexandra Amalie of Bavaria (b. 1826) who believed that her body contained a grand piano made of glass.

undulatus asperitas

This newly observed cloud formation is yet to enter the *International Cloud Atlas*.

The Flower Remedies

The poems are based on the remedies created by Dr Bach in the 1930s. In each poem, the plant or flower is imagined to be afflicted with the difficulty for which it is a remedy.